T H E   M A K I N G   O F

EVITA

by A L A N   P A R K E R

Introduction by M A D O N N A

Photographs from the film by D A V I D   A P P L E B Y

Cinematography by D A R I U S   K H O N D J I

Book design by E R B E   D E S I G N ,   L O S   A N G E L E S

CollinsPublishers
A Division of HarperCollins*Publishers*

First published in 1996 by
Collins Publishers
The Making of Evita.
Design and compilation copyright
©1996 by Collins Publishers.
All rights reserved.
Text and photographs copyright
©1996 by Cinergi Pictures
Entertainment Inc. and Cinergi
Productions N.V. Inc. All rights
reserved.

Text by: ALAN PARKER
Introduction by: MADONNA
Photographs by: DAVID APPLEBY
Editor: JAIN LEMOS
Art Director: ALAN PARKER
Photo Editor: LISA MORAN
Designers: MAUREEN ERBE,
    RITA A. SOWINS
    ERBE DESIGN, LOS ANGELES

First Edition

ISBN 0-00-649100-6 (paperback)
ISBN 0-00-649095-6 (hardcover)

P

Introduction erhaps to some people this is just a picture book. A collection of photographs taken on the set of a movie. But to me, it's a testament of the blood, sweat, and tears that were shed by many to make this film a reality. A collective map of many hearts that were squeezed and wrenched, trampled and twisted, and often pushed to the breaking point. ⚜ I had no idea what I was in for when I was asked to be in this movie, but I soon realized that there was no middle ground. No playing it safe. It was sink or swim for everyone. We all took chances and we all made sacrifices. Not just the actors and actresses but the grips and the sparks and the cinematographer and the camera operator and the hair and makeup department and the set designer and the choreographer and I could go on and on. ⚜ We flew halfway around the world enduring blistering heat and bone-chilling cold. We witnessed political uprisings and scathing media attacks. We worked in countries we were not welcome in and watched while angry slogans were painted on walls telling us to "Get Out!" We pissed off presidents and bishops and probably a few studio executives as well. We crawled into bed at night wondering if there was ever going to be an end to the madness and at one time or another we all wanted to quit. But we didn't. ⚜ What kept us hanging on? Was it the music of Andrew Lloyd Webber and Tim Rice that took hold of us and wouldn't let go? Was it Alan Parker who marched forward like a visionary pied piper, daring us to follow him? Or was it Evita herself who crept into our dreams at night and cast a magic spell on all of us? Who knows? What's important is that we survived. ⚜ We created something rare and beautiful and our lives will never be the same. ⚜ Of course this book won't tell you everything and it won't ever be as exciting as watching the film, but I can't hold a movie in my hands and press it to my heart. I can't show it to my daughter while she's sitting on my knee. And when I'm a very old woman, tired and bent with arthritis, maybe I won't want to get out of my rocking chair and go to the movies. Maybe I'll just want to look at the book . ⚜ Maybe you will too. — M A D O N N A

THE MAKING *of* THE FILM
by ALAN PARKER

ABOVE: *Director Alan Parker*

"It's not easy making movies and it's certainly not glamorous.
The manic, tormented hard work, the long, upside-down hours,
and being constantly ankle deep in pig shit is the reality.
But sometimes it's really worth it."

Someone once said, "He who leaps into the void owes no explanation to those who stand and watch." To try to describe how *Evita* was made into a film fills me with some trepidation, as the pictures you see in this book probably should be explanation enough. As, indeed, *should* be a viewing of the actual movie. One of the difficulties a film maker has in any explication of the nuts and bolts and *Sturm und Drang* of making a film is that the chronological order of the story (and of the photographs in this book) bears no resemblance to the lunatic logic of how things were actually achieved. But I will attempt to start from the beginning.

The common claim from most people who write about Argentina is that an objective historical perspective runs counter to Argentinean culture, particularly when it comes to the passions they have for and against Eva and Juan Perón. It seems that the personal memories that historians rely on are partisan at least and fragile at most. Also, the miserable political legacy of years of interrupted democracy and numerous military dictatorships have played havoc with the reliability, or even existence, of historical documentation.

In his excellent essay, *The Return Of Eva Perón*, V.S. Naipaul quotes a poem by Jorge Luis Borges (an anti-Peronist) which describes more eloquently Argentina's national selective memory:

> *A cigar store perfumed the desert like a rose.*
> *The afternoon had established its yesterdays,*
> *And men took on together an illusory past.*
> *Only one thing was missing—the street had no other side.*

So how does one go about making a balanced and accurate film on Eva Perón when myth and reality collide at every turn of her story? Many saw her as a lady bountiful, champion of the disenfranchised, nothing less than a saint. Others saw her as an opportunistic, meretricious, conniving devil incarnate. Eva called herself "a sparrow in a great flock of sparrows." Her supporters called her "the Lady of Hope" and her detractors, "the charming child with a loaded gun."

This dichotomy was reflected in the reaction to the original musical. On one side of the divide, Tim Rice had acknowledged the importance of Mary Main's (Maria Flores) book, *Evita: The Woman With The Whip*, as being important in his research. Maria Flores was an Anglo-Argentine historical novelist who, it has been contended since, drew her information mostly from the opposition and oligarchy, and hence her book (published in 1955 and subsequently often quoted by detractors) was little more than anti-Peronist gossip. On the other side of the divide, the anti-Evita camp equally saw the musical as Eva's unwarranted glorification. (Including, it has to be said, the subsequent military dictatorships which banned all performances of *Evita* and the importation of the record.)

How can you accurately describe a woman whose image has been used as a flag by both left-wing guerrillas and right-wing extremists?

With this disclaimer, I humbly offer a very short history of Eva Perón (along with the captions that accompany the photos in this book), which is reflected in my film.

Eva Perón was born María Eva Ibarguren, the youngest illegitimate daughter of Juan Duarte, a middle-class *estancia* manager, and a domestic servant, Juana Ibarguren, on May 7, 1919, in Los Toldos, a tiny dot on the map lost in the vast Pampas two hundred miles west of Buenos Aires. Seven years later, Juan Duarte died in a car crash and his Ibarguren family was prevented from attending the funeral by Duarte's legal wife, Doña Estela Grisolía. (The painful rejection that young Eva and her mother suffered here stayed with her all of her life. She would often refer to it, and the event formed the basis of her often fanatical hatred of Argentina's middle and upper classes.)

Doña Juana later moved her family to the nearby town of Junín, where she opened a boarding house. It was here, at the age of fifteen, that Eva met Agustín Magaldi, the dubiously talented tango singer whom she persuaded to take her back to Buenos Aires. Whether Magaldi discarded Eva or she him gets lost in conjecture and the cigar smoke Jorge Luis Borges mentions above. As do the details of her early years in Buenos Aires, as she bounced from lover to lover in an indisputably male-dominated society, prior to her minor celebrity as a film and radio actress.

Eva first met Colonel Juan Perón (see page 43) on January 22, 1944, at a charity concert organized to aid victims of the San Juan earthquake. Soon openly living with Perón as his mistress, she attracted the displeasure of both the oligarchy—the ruling class—and Perón's military cohorts. Disturbed by his growing public popularity, the ruling junta subsequently arrested Perón and incarcerated him at Martín García Island prison. The populist insurrection that followed on October 17, 1945, led to his release and free elections the following year, which Perón won comfortably, becoming the 29th president of Argentina. Eva threw herself into life as Argentina's first lady with a media blitz common now but unheard of then. She visited Spain, Italy and France as part of her "Rainbow Tour" of Europe, and her movie-star style and populist charisma propelled her to worldwide celebrity. The global media exposure established her as one of the most famous women in the world and, certainly, the most famous woman ever to come out of South America.

Returning to Argentina from Europe, and perhaps chastened by her frivolous image and her husband's dubious politics (as viewed in the West), Eva threw herself into "good works." She created her own charitable organization, *La Fundación Ayuda Social María Eva Duarte de Perón*, and proceeded to work sixteen-hour days righting the wrongs, as she saw them, in Argentina's unequal society. She oversaw the opening of twelve new hospitals and a thousand new schools (all conveniently—and confusingly—named after her), clinics, medical centers, homes for the aged, homes for single girls, convalescent centers and shelters for the homeless. She even built an entire miniature children's city, *La Ciudad Infantil*, many years before Walt Disney came up with the idea. She gave away 200,000 cooking pots to the poor, 400,000 pairs of shoes, 500,000 sewing machines, and so the list goes on. In a stroke of bravado, she even sent medical supplies and clothing to help the poor of the United States. Her generosity and demagoguery knew no end, except for the final bill. The country was slowly becoming bankrupt. Whether due to Eva's extravagant beneficence or her husband's shaky, autocratic economic policies, or because the Peróns were just plain stealing, the truth is lost in Borges' cigar smoke and the contradictions of many historians. When asked by an American journalist why she didn't keep books for her charitable efforts, Eva replied, "Keeping books on charity is capitalist nonsense. I just use money for the poor. I can't stop to count it."

Eva's celebrity and political clout were consolidated in the creation of the Peronist Women's Party (Eva campaigned for women's right to vote and it had become law in 1947). As her popular support grew, so did the dissident voices. Her ruthlessness and despotic fanaticism toward achieving her goals made her many enemies, not least of all within Peron's military. The nervous generals at the Campo de Mayo garrison saw her aspirations to the vice-presidency as nothing short of heresy. Eva was put forward as the vice-presidential candidate by the five-million-strong General Confederation of Labor (CGT), which organized the mammoth rally of August 22, 1951, that filled the *Avenida 9 de julio* with a million supporters. The CGT had erected a giant, five-story-high scaffolding edifice to house the speaking platform. A massive arch framed the podium, declaring *"Perón-Eva Perón,*

La Formula de la Patria," and the huge crowd clamored for her to accept the vice-presidential nomination.

But their efforts were all for nothing. Nine days later, everything changed. Eva made an emotional, tearful radio broadcast renouncing all of her political ambitions. What caused this sudden reversal is not clear. Whether it was pressure on Perón from the military, or whether the medical diagnosis of her uterine cancer had finally been made clear to her, or perhaps some other factor, no one has ever explained to this writer. I have read 29 books on the subject, and asked the question of almost everyone I met in Argentina, of people who knew her, people who loved her, people who hated her, without receiving satisfactory explanation. Once again, the truth vanishes in a cloud of Argentine cigar smoke.

For eleven months, Argentina witnessed Eva's slow and public dying. In the elections of November, 1951, a special ballot box was brought to her bedside for her to cast her vote (and for her to be photographed for the Peronist media machine). For Perón's second term inaugural motorcade in June of 1952, emaciated and heavily sedated, she had to be propped up by a steel cage which was hidden from the crowds by her ample fur coat.

At 8:25 PM on July 26, 1952, Eva died.

❧

If the reason for this film is Eva Perón, its genesis as a creative work, of course, resides with Tim Rice and Andrew Lloyd Webber. Tim was the first to be taken by the idea of a modern, sung-through opera on the life of Evita. A one-line synopsis of her rags-to-riches story and tragic early death is not just the stuff of musical theater or the Hollywood dream machine, but also has resonance in the classic operas from *Tristan und Isolde* to *La Bohème*. Tim and Andrew had originally conceived and executed it as a complete, cohesive and conceptual recording before it was performed on stage (as they had done with their previous collaboration, *Jesus Christ Superstar*). The album was released in Britain in November of 1976, and the single release of "Don't Cry For Me Argentina," sung by Julie Covington, had gone to number one in the British charts a month earlier.

My initial personal involvement with the project began soon after the album came out. I had inquired of their manager, David Land, if they had thought of making a film of the record, being as it was for all to hear (and see) completely cinematic. I was told that "the boys" wanted to put it on stage first, and so I bowed out gracefully. Hal Prince had been persuaded by Andrew to direct the show and it opened to great success in London in June 1978, with Elaine Paige as Evita. The show subsequently transferred to Broadway in 1979 starring Patti LuPone, where, despite mixed reviews, it ironically won the New York Drama Critics Circle Award for Best Musical and seven Tonys, running for 1,567 performances.

I had the pleasure of being invited to the Broadway opening by the producer, Robert Stigwood. Robert asked me if I would like to make a film of *Evita* and I told him I'd give him my answer when I had finished my film *Fame*, which I was then shooting in New York. After completing *Fame* and while enjoying some rest on the Caribbean island of St. Maarten, I received a call from Robert, who said he was steaming toward the island in his yacht. After a day of sumptuous hospitality on his boat, the like of which no mortal but Robert can provide, he asked me if I wanted to play tennis. Forever the dutiful guest, I obliged, and the two of us were whisked across the bay in one of his launches to a nearby hotel tennis court, where we disembarked and watched the launch speed back to the yacht. The problem was that the tennis court was locked. Robert and I, now completely stranded, walked down the dusty main street. Finally, out of the blue, he said, "So, are you going to make *Evita* or not?" I mumbled that after *Fame* I didn't want to do back-to-back musicals, and so my answer was no. Robert said nothing for a while, and then suddenly started bashing me with his tennis racket. I ran back to my hotel. This is a true story.

For fifteen years I watched as the film of *Evita* was *about* to be made, and the various press releases were printed in the media. I have been furnished with the various news clippings from those years, and would first like to mention the stars that would supposedly be starring in the film. They include: Elaine Paige, Patti LuPone, Charo, Raquel Welch, Ann-Margret, Bette Midler, Meryl Streep, Barbra Streisand, Liza Minnelli, Diane Keaton, Olivia Newton-John, Elton John, John Travolta, Pia Zadora, Meat Loaf, Elliott Gould, Sylvester Stallone, Barry Gibb, Cyndi Lauper, Gloria Estefan, Mariah Carey, Jeremy Irons, Raul Julia and Michelle Pfeiffer. And then there were the directors: Ken Russell, Herb Ross, Alan Pakula, Hector Babenco, Francis Coppola, Franco Zeffirelli, Michael Cimino, Richard Attenborough, Glenn Gordon Caron and Oliver Stone. So why didn't it get made until now? And with none of the individuals mentioned above? I'm sure I don't know. All I do know is that all those years, I sort of regretted saying no to Robert in that dusty street. So I was glad that everything came full circle when Andy Vajna and his company, Cinergi, finally did have the courage to finance the film, and asked me to direct it at the end of 1994.

When I began work on the film, the incumbent actress to play Evita was Michelle Pfeiffer. She had waited such a long time to do the film that she had even had a baby in the meantime. I met with Michelle, whom I greatly admire, and it was clear that with two small children she wasn't about to embark on the long Lewis and Clark journey I had in mind—a long way from the comfort of nearby Hollywood sound stages. While spending Christmas in England in 1994, I received out of the blue a letter from Madonna. (I had developed a remake of *The Blue Angel* with her some years previously, but it had bitten the Hollywood dust.) Her handwritten, four-page letter was extraordinarily passionate and sincere. As far as she was concerned, no one could play Evita as well as she could, and she said that she would sing, dance and act her heart out, and put *everything* else on hold to devote all her time to it should I decide to go with her. And that's exactly what she did do. (Well, she didn't put *everything* on hold, as she did get pregnant before we finished filming.)

Antonio Banderas was already the favorite to play Ché. I viewed a tape of him singing in a cold audition he had done years before, and I was easily convinced. I flew to Miami where he was filming and had dinner with him as he sang aloud (to the surprised pleasure of the surrounding tables) every song from the show, which he already knew by heart—even the songs his character, Ché, doesn't sing in the movie.

For Perón, I decided on Jonathan Pryce. Apart from being a brilliant, classically trained British actor, he had also created the lead role of "The Engineer" in the stage musical *Miss Saigon*, for which he won a Tony Award. I had also most recently seen his bravura performance as Lytton Strachey in *Carrington*. Jonathan, although taken by the script, first wanted to meet with me before he committed. As he was on holiday in France at the time, I flew to see him at Marseilles airport, where it had been arranged by his London agent that we could conveniently have our meeting. Unfortunately, Jonathan's New York agent thought it unwise, and told him *not* to go, neglecting to tell me that the meeting was canceled. I consequently spent four hours in the Marseilles airport arrivals hall, lugging around a very heavy carrier bag of research material on Juan Perón, drinking many cups of coffee and glasses of Pastis while chasing after every tall, English-looking man that I could find before getting the evening plane back to London. (I'm pleased to say that Jonathan no longer has that New York agent.) Finally, we did meet back in London and he was on board.

My initial priority had been to write my screenplay. Armed with every filmed documentary made on Eva Perón, every possible book in the English language on the Peróns and Argentina, and any old news cuttings I could get my hands on, I did my research. When Tim did his original libretto there was very little for him to work from, but ironically the success of the musical had spawned many biographies. My intention was to write a balanced story, as thoroughly researched as possible, inspired always by the heart of the original piece, which was Andrew's score and Tim's lyrics. I ignored the stage play completely, as the theatrical decisions that Hal Prince made bore little relevance to a cinematic interpretation. And so I went back to the original concept album from which I had wanted to make a film eighteen years previously.

In the stage version, Hal Prince had insisted that Ché, the Brechtian, everyman narrator, be clearly identified as Ché Guevara (complete with beard, beret and fatigues) for its obvious, immediate stage effect. My own script refers to him merely as "Ché" (a common nickname in Argentina, like "buddy" is in the U.S.) Suffice it to say that Ernesto "Ché" Guevara, born in Rosario, Argentina, in 1928, almost certainly never met Eva Perón. He entered Buenos Aires University in 1948 to study medicine, and qualified as a doctor a year after Eva's death. When the musical was written, Guevara, a revolutionary, iconoclastic presence which had adorned many a bedroom wall in the 60s (including my own), was still relevant, and the coincidence of his Argentinean birth became an excellent theatrical device around which Tim Rice could construct his libretto. My own feeling was that Ché Guevara's actual story should not be cosmetically or dishonestly grafted onto ours. Indeed, it probably deserved a film or two of its own. And it wasn't to be this one. Hence the narrator in my film is purely and simply "Ché."

By May of 1995, I had finished writing my script—which called for 146 changes to the original score and lyrics—and so, like a mailman offering his leg to a couple of hungry Rottweilers, I sent my first draft to Andrew and Tim. Fortunately, they liked it very much. The next step was for the three of us to get together. It's no secret that Andrew and Tim no longer have a comfortable working relationship, having chosen not to collaborate for many years. Consequently it was obvious that getting the two of them together in the same room to go through the new work was going to be no easy task. After a great deal of the tangoing and juggling of schedules that the two of them are famous for, Tim and I flew to Andrew's house in the South of France, and with me as piggy in the middle, worked solidly—and surprisingly productively—addressing my 146 music notes. One of the many changes I had made was to rearrange the order of most of the last act, eliminating the prolonged recitative of the original. This called for new scoring from Andrew and, most important, a new song to be written by the two of them. For obvious reasons, Andrew doesn't give his melodies away too hastily, and the possibility of these two gentlemen ever collaborating again was, I was told by many who knew them well, an idealistic but not overly practical notion.

In New York, Madonna had begun work with the esteemed vocal coach Joan Lader. She was determined to sing the demanding score as Andrew had written it, and not to cheat in any way. Within three months she expanded her vocal range, finding parts of her voice that she had never used before in her own songs. She had also learned the *Evita* score from our musical supervisor David Caddick, who has worked with Andrew for many years as musical director on his shows.

In September, Madonna, Antonio Banderas, Jonathan Pryce and Jimmy Nail (who plays tango singer Agustín Magaldi) began rehearsals with me in London. My approach to this unusual film genre—being as it is a completely sung-through piece with no con-

ventional dialogue—I was convinced should be as naturalistic as possible, its only theatricality being the fact that it's sung and not spoken. Any other choices made I felt should be the same as if I were doing a normal dramatic film. To this end, Madonna dragged Jimmy around the studio, bashing him with her suitcase as we enacted the scenes as they were written in the script. Mindful of the fact that Jimmy, in his youth, was once in prison for causing grievous bodily harm, I feared for the consequences. However, he was a paragon of English good manners, quietly suffering the bruises inflicted on him. Rumor has it that Jimmy, an avid Newcastle United football fanatic, perhaps only did the film because he thought Maradonna was in it. (For those not so fanatical about football, Maradonna is the great Argentinean soccer player.)

By October 2, we were ready to begin recording in London. Our first day at CTS Studios in Wembley, it has to be said, was a complete nightmare (what came to be known amongst us as "Black Monday"). David Caddick had, probably idealistically, suggested that we begin with "Don't Cry For Me Argentina," with Madonna laying down a guide vocal simultaneously with an 84-piece orchestra. Andrew attended this recording session and, frankly, was soon apoplectic about everything from the playing of the instruments to the conductor, to the engineer, to the way the orchestra was configured in the studio, to the closeness of the violins to the studio wall. Madonna equally hated the experience, and was close to tears as she wondered, with due cause, what the hell she had gotten herself into. The cozy, creative recording environment she was used to was light-years away from this frenetic musical madhouse as the worlds of musical theater, film and recording were suddenly colliding. It was obvious that I had to put things right.

At the end of the day, ironically, we all gathered in an adjacent studio for a photo call to announce the commencement of recording. Our cheesy smiles belied what we were really feeling as we all put on brave and professional faces as the hundreds of cameras rattled away. That evening, I followed Andrew's car home and we had dinner in an Italian restaurant near his house. The conversation was heated while the food got cold, but we finally reached positive creative conclusions as, I have to say, we have on every occasion since. I suggested that Andrew and I go round immediately to Madonna's hotel to talk to her, which we duly did. Between the three of us, we decided how to proceed. Andrew had suggested that we ask the celebrated American conductor John Mauceri to come to London to conduct our large orchestra sessions. Madonna, Caddick, myself and Madonna's vocal engineer would continue all the vocals at Whitfield Street Studios, a contemporary music studio, the ambience of which was more conducive to the job at hand. Madonna would sing in the afternoons, every other day, to save and strengthen her voice, and Nigel Wright, the music producer who had worked extensively with Andrew, would, with Caddick and myself, fill the remaining recording time preparing the multitude of other tracks needed. By the end of the week, the maestro Mauceri had performed his magic with a brilliant catchment of the finest orchestral players in London and all thoughts of Black Monday were forgotten. We were on our way.

Everything we recorded was done with the naturalistic philosophy mentioned previously. As we were going to film nearly all the scenes to prerecorded playback, decisions had to be made in the recording studio that I was going to have to live with during filming. Ever mindful of this, I sat every day with my script in my lap fielding all the questions the actors would ask. In a way, *Evita* was like making two films, one first in a recording studio and one later with a camera on a film set. Over a period of four months, working seven days a week, we put in over 400 recording hours preparing the 49 musical sections that were required for playback on set. But we still didn't have our new song.

ABOVE: *Young Eva with her mother, Doña Juana Ibarguren,*
and sisters Blanca and Elisa, attempting to attend the funeral of Eva's father.
Doña Juana is prevented from entering the church by Duarte's legal wife, Doña Estela Grisolía.

Finally, while I was visiting Andrew at his country estate in Berkshire to play him the tracks we had recorded, he suddenly sat down at the piano and played the most beautiful melody, which he suggested could be our new song. Needless to say, I grabbed it. However, we still needed lyrics, so Tim dutifully began to put words to the music. The vast majority of the original *Evita* score had been done this way: music first, lyrics afterwards. After many weeks of nail biting, Tim was finally cajoled into writing the lyrics that now accompany the music to "You Must Love Me." Tim also completely rewrote the lyrics of "The Lady's Got Potential," which Antonio sings. (This song, from the original album, had been dropped by Hal Prince for the stage version, and I had resurrected it for my screenplay in order to tell the history of Argentine politics which preceded the Perón presidency.)

Having devoted so much time to the recording, it was vital to return to my "day job" of being a film director, as every department was screaming for my attention. Earlier, in June of 1995, with the help of the State Department and Senator Dodd of Connecticut, I had been granted an audience with Argentina's President Carlos Menem. I quickly got on a plane to Buenos Aires and the following day was at the President's private residence, Los Olivos. Swarming with dark-suited security people with walkie-talkies and dark glasses, my first impression was that I was visiting Marlon Brando at the Corleone compound in New Jersey. The President was gracious and polite, but as a Peronist he was obviously concerned that the memory of Eva Perón be respected. Also, because of previous attempts to film *Evita* in Argentina, I was walking into a political hothouse due to Oliver Stone's public utterances when he was seeking permission to film there. Oliver's manner is not always the material of diplomacy, and this was not the first time I've had to apologize for him. The bottom line was that I wanted their cooperation, and most of all the use of the Casa Rosada, the official government house which figures so importantly in our story. I promised Menem respect and accuracy, but reserved my right as an artist to make the film that I saw fit. I told him that I wouldn't be giving them a script to vet, and that there would undoubtedly be parts of the film that he would disagree with. By attempting a balanced view of Eva Perón, I obviously couldn't please everyone, especially in such a partisan country as Argentina. As I sat talking to the President, I noticed that to one side of the desk was a very large portrait of Eva Perón, and to the other side a sizable religious statue of *the* Madonna. Unable to take my eyes off this statue, I began to get nervous that he might ask me who was going to play the eponymous role.

The President concluded the meeting by saying that he was proud of Argentina's fledgling democracy and therefore he couldn't say "yes" or "no" to me making the film, but he surely would have a couple of million Peronistas on his back if he granted me use of the Casa Rosada, and anyway, in the nearly hundred years since it was built, no one had ever filmed there. Would Queen Elizabeth allow me to film in Buckingham Palace? I lamely answered that no one would want to. He closed the meeting, enigmatically changing the subject by asking me if I would check out the new Dolby sound system in his screening room. I obeyed. It sounded fine, although I've heard that he recently installed digital equipment in anticipation of screening *Evita*. Outside the gates of Los Olivos, I encountered fifty newspeople anxious to know what had happened in our meeting. As I had been told to keep our encounter a secret, I was a little taken aback by the microphones being stuffed through the open car window and indeed that the media had been alerted. It was a first lesson of how things work in Argentina.

It was obvious to me that because of the strong feelings for and against Eva Perón in Argentina, no sensible planning could be done as one would do on a normal movie. As discouraged as I was, I still wanted to make at least *part* of the film in Argentina, even though it was

apparent that it would be impractical, if not dangerous, to shoot everything there. This country is the spiritual heart of the film—a strange, fascinating place that would be difficult, if not impossible, to replicate completely elsewhere. Unlike any other South American country, Argentina prides itself on its "European-ness," settled as it was by Italians and Spanish with pockets of British, French and Germans. There are half a million Jews and as many Arabs among the population. They say that you can push a plow westward from Buenos Aires across the rich, fertile Pampas for a thousand miles and never hit a stone. There are the tropical Iguasso falls in the north and Antarctic glaciers to the south. From the vineyards of Córdoba to the rocky expanse of Patagonia, the country is truly unique. I'm sure I'm not the first Englishman to be taken by the strange, paradoxical and incomprehensible beauty of it all.

Even if we only filmed there for a few weeks, I was determined to shoot *something* in Argentina. I had visited Eva's birthplace of Los Toldos, the town of Junín where she grew up, and Chivilcoy where her father's funeral took place. At the very least, I would shoot these scenes of Eva's early life there.

I then visited seven other countries before determining a strategy. I decided to start filming in Buenos Aires, and then move to Budapest, where I thought we could accurately replicate the once beautiful European architecture of Buenos Aires in the thirties and forties, which has since been decimated and replaced by hideous and mindless structures. (Filming any historical recreation of this nature would have been difficult even with complete cooperation.) Whether our stay in Buenos Aires would be shorter or longer than two weeks depended on those irate Peronistas who thought our project heretical and Madonna unsuitable to play their *Santa Evita*.

Our crew was principally English, but we had American, French, Scottish and Irish technicians too. We freighted more than 70 tons of equipment from England and by mid-January our traveling crew of 90 was ensconced in Buenos Aires for our preparations, hopefully to begin filming on February 8. When I arrived at Buenos Aires' Ezeiza airport, the hoards of journalists and TV cameras that swamped me with questions was a presage of what was to come. On the drive in to the city, I gulped as I saw the hand-painted graffiti on every bridge and sizable wall that screamed out: "*Fuera* (go home) *Madonna,*" "*Viva Evita,*" and "*Chau Alan Parker and your English task force.*" (During the Falklands War, the British troops were referred to as the "Task Force.")

At the time, I remember squeezing my eyes closed and thinking: a) I've made a terrible mistake bringing Madonna, Antonio and everyone else into this nightmare; b) If I squeeze my eyes even tighter, it will all be over and I'll be at the wrap party in London. The angry messages were all signed by a group called "The Commandos of the Peronista." I made one hopeful observation that the lettering on the dozens of signs was identical and that "Task Force" was always misspelled "*Taks* Force." With perhaps foolish optimism, I suspected that it might all be the work of just one dyslexic commando.

Once in Buenos Aires for the duration, my immediate job at hand was to cast the scores of smaller parts and to finalize our dozens of locations. As we were ferried from location to location we were stalked by convoys of paparazzi, who at the time had more cameras than we did. Wherever they got the misguided notion that any movie star would bother to go on a location scout, I'll never know.

Also, I took the time to absorb my script and think about just how I was going to film this behemoth. The final weeks just before shooting are always a nerve-wracking time for any director, but for the first time, I was more than nervous—I was truly fearful. The enormity of this film and the daunting logistics were burden enough on top of our obvious security concerns.

ABOVE: *Young Eva
is prevented from laying flowers
on her father's corpse
by members of the Duarte family.*

RIGHT: *Pages from
Alan Parker's shooting script.*

6. INT.   CHIVILCOY   CHURCH   DAY

Close on the dead man's face. Young Eva walks up and places
her small bouquet of flowers onto the corpse. She stretches
to kiss her father, but is grabbed by the Duarte mourners.   Music 4

We hear 'Evita! Evita! Evita!' from the 'Requiem' as young
Eva is dragged off, kicking and screaming.

YOUNG EVA

Papa! Papa! He's my Papa!

On her crying face - and suddenly a giant surge in the music
as we cut on the swell of the 'Requiem' to:

BUENOS AIRES AVENIDA, 1952   DAY

7. EXT.

The funeral of Eva Perón. Colossal. All the trappings of
state: MILITARY and the mourning THOUSANDS. A massive,
macabre orgy of collective national grief.

We see a black, bulbous, silver-trimmed cedar coffin draped
with the blue-and-white Argentine flag. It sits atop an iron-
wheeled gun carriage which is pulled, with ropes, by 39 men
and women in white shirts and black trousers, skirts: the
uniform of Eva's 'descamisados'.

The silver-trimmed coffin mounted on a gun carriage was pulled by men and women from the CGT (Confederación General del Trabajo —the Federation of Labor), dressed in the white shirts of Eva's *descamisados*. Attended by two million, with all the trappings of state—including 17,000 military— the funeral was a massive, macabre display of collective national grief. Some saw this "frenzy of sorrow" as a genuine, spontaneous demonstration, others called it a "bacchanal of necrophilia."

Madonna arrived early in Buenos Aires to do her own research and to continue her fittings for the 80-odd costume changes she has in the film. She was naturally upset by the unwelcoming signs that greeted her, but her greatest immediate problem was the crowd of fans and paparazzi camped outside her hotel keeping her awake at night and restricting her movements. She had made her own contacts and began a slew of meetings with elderly Peronistas and also anti-Peronists as she gathered her own personal research on Eva. Meanwhile, I continued my diplomatic tangos with cabinet members, ambassadors, government officials and army generals with regard to our quest for the balcony of the Casa Rosada and the many other locations for which we needed permission. Although all of them gave me the party line—fearful as they were of the extreme Evita-ists in the Peronist party—I never gave up hope, although, sensibly, maybe I should have. Apart from the historical importance of the actual Casa Rosada balcony, "Don't Cry For Me Argentina" is the heart of the score and the most well known "scene." I made it clear that we had made contingency plans to build the entire facade at Shepperton Studios in England. My production designer, Brian Morris, had already photographed every square inch of the Casa Rosada and his construction manager had been moved on by military guards a dozen times whilst measuring up with his tape. In other words, I was going to shoot the Casa Rosada whether they gave me permission to use theirs or not. The pro-Peronist press attacked us daily, even though they had no knowledge of what we were doing, and the news clippings piled higher and higher from around the world as we read about how unwelcome we were in Argentina. There was nothing to do but take it on the chin and forge onwards.

With our core crew of 90 and over 150 additional Argentinean crew members, we were a small, self-contained army, and our juggernaut just rolled onwards. Most of my crew had worked on many of my previous films, but it was the first time I had worked with the cinematographer Darius Khondji. Darius, a Frenchman of Persian descent, I once described as a cross between Pierre-Auguste Renoir and Fernandel. His continual brilliance (and shadows) and affable personality made the filming a constant delight, as he integrated perfectly with my usual camera crew. Except that he was French. As in, "Darius, why have you ordered all these dogs?" as I inquired testily one day at the Buenos Aires dockside. "Dogs?" he replied. "Yes, dogs. The art department have delivered 20 poodles." He shrugged his shoulders in the way that only the French can. "No, I asked for poodles, like when it rains." The assistant directors and I countered in unison, "You mean puddles." He stared at us as if we were mad, "Yes, poodles."

Through the streets of Buenos Aires and the Pampas beyond, the paparazzi and sleaze journalists from around the world continued to follow us everywhere, sidling up to crew members with a hope of digging up some dirt on Madonna or Antonio, but they gradually grew despondent as it dawned on them that we were just making a movie. And, maybe, a good one.

There was no way that we could keep them away, as we were filming out in the open. We recreated the Buenos Aires streets that Eva first encountered in 1936, involving period vehicles, thousands of costumed extras, and entire street-lengths of art direction. No easy task in the center of a busy city of ten million people. (Although we did film on Sundays, when most Buenos Aires *Porteños*—and the paparazzi—were either in church or, mostly, sleeping off their very late Saturday nights.)

Fed up one day with being constantly buzzed by paparazzi helicopters whilst we were filming, I made a rude gesture into the sky. The next day, *Crónica*, the extremist daily, ran a picture of me, on the end of a 1000mm lens, flipping my finger with a caption declaring my disrespect for Eva Perón. The press madness culminated for me during a visit I made to the men's room of the Marriott hotel after returning from a hard night's work in La Boca (the crazy—and dangerous—dockside area of Buenos Aires). As I stood at the urinal, a journalist rushed in and positioned himself next to me. I modestly hunched over for a little privacy as the gentleman brandished his tape recorder in front of my face with one hand whilst he unzipped his fly with the other. He jabbered something like, "What did you think of the disgraceful sex whore playing the part of Madonna?" I wasn't quite sure what he meant, as he obviously hadn't got past his first Berlitz tape. "She'll do just great," I offered, knowing that the sound of my voice wouldn't be heard on the tape over his very loud peeing. As he continued to jabber away, I just shrugged my shoulders to be left alone and finally he rushed out, as if he had obtained some scoop. I could see the headline in *Crónica*: "Scandal! Parker confirms worst fears: Madonna will be played by Madonna." As I washed my hands, wondering how much crazier all this could get, I suddenly heard a cellular phone ring in one of the adjacent lavatory stalls. Behind the closed door I heard the occupant answer, as he pulled at the toilet roll, "Yes. No. Parker won't talk. But listen, I just overheard him doing an interview." The weeks went by, our cameras kept rolling, and the fans, politicians, journalists, paparazzi and flag-burning, wall-painting "commandos" bothered us less and less as our endeavors came to be embraced by the public at large (especially the many whom we employed).

Whether because of this attrition or some other reason, things suddenly turned for the better. Madonna, through her network of Peronist elderlies, had managed an unofficial, personal meeting with Menem. Madonna and I were having one of our regular script meetings when she got the call. As she dashed out the door, I told her to take her CD of "Don't Cry For Me" with her, and she rushed off to meet the President. In her one-hour meeting, Madonna probably achieved more than the rest of us—skiing on the diplomatic treacle—had done in nearly a year. A week later, we were summoned to an official meeting with the President. Jonathan, Antonio, Madonna and myself sat on one side of a large table at Los Olivos nibbling the President's famous pizza. After much small talk and diplomatic tap dancing, Madonna suddenly said to the President, "Let's cut to the chase here. Do we have the balcony or don't we?" Menem smiled and nodded, "You can have the balcony."

Soon after, utilizing every lamp, banner and costume that we had with us, we were filming in front of the Casa Rosada with 4,000 extras. When Madonna came out onto the balcony and began singing "Don't Cry For Me Argentina," the crowd went crazy, as did all of the crew. On the second night of shooting there, as we filmed the reverses on the crowd, I stood with Madonna on the balcony. With all of the documentary footage imprinted in the back of our brains, it was impossible not to be moved when we were standing in the same spot where Eva stood looking down at a crowd of adoring thousands. Suddenly it wasn't just the illusion and replication of film. It was strangely real. We shot throughout the night, and as the sun came up in the morning, we all quietly hugged one another. I think we all felt that we had, in five weeks, done all that we had set out to do and more. We had overcome the media bombardment, even as many wished—and expected—us to fail. I felt that I had captured the heart of our story on film and we were leaving with, albeit guarded, a sense of triumph. It's not easy making movies and it's certainly not glamorous. The manic, tormented hard work, the long, upside-down hours, and being constantly ankle-deep in pig shit is the reality. But sometimes it's really worth it.

The irony occurred to me, during one particularly sweaty and arduous day's filming, that we were working fourteen-hour days, six days a week, sometimes seven, to make a film about a woman who fought for a five-day week for working people.

And so we moved to Hungary. David Lean said that film crews are the last of the traveling circuses, and that's what we were when all of us, plus tons of equipment, costumes and props, were transported to Budapest and were up and running and shooting in four days. Madonna had gone to New York for a break before joining us, and it was from there that she phoned me. "Are you sitting down, Alan?. . . I'm pregnant." "How much?" "When is it due?" The calculations of shooting days left buzzed through my head as I tried not to panic. To begin with, we were going to keep it a secret, but the Kafka-esque conversations that I began to have about our schedule with David Wimbury, the line producer, and Dennis Maguire, the first assistant director, defied all logic as they started to wonder if I had finally lost my marbles. It was obvious that Madonna had to make her announcement, and she did.

But there were other obstacles to overcome. I have to be honest that the crew, actors and myself were not taken by Hungary. The inherent misery of the place and the people were a far cry from the pleasure and wide Latin smiles we had left in Argentina. Frankly, Hungary is a very frustrating place. First, as noticed by others before me, the blue Danube is not blue, but decidedly brown. The food, like so much else, is a dreadful legacy of communist austerity and a more traditional, cholesterol-packed kamikaze dive into an early death. When we arrived, shooting mainly outdoors, we thankfully had no snow, but it was terribly cold. And then the unique Budapest cold/hot weather collision hit us. For some geographic reason, there is no spring in Hungary. The Nazis and Russians didn't steal it, as they stole everything else from this sad country—Budapest never had one. As all students of communism know, nearby Prague has a spring, but not Budapest. The sudden peculiar rise in barometric pressure gave the crew headaches and nosebleeds and they suddenly turned cranky. (Istvan Szabo, the great Hungarian director, visited the set and told me to be wary of these "crazy weeks," when apparently many Hungarians end up divorced, in jail, in an asylum or jumping off the Liberty Bridge into the solace of the brown Danube.)

Our biggest work in Hungary was to prepare and film Eva Perón's state funeral. We had analyzed the documentary footage of the actual mammoth event and were anxious to replicate it down to the smallest details. To be ready for filming on the first shooting day, the costume department began fitting and dressing the extras at 3:30 AM. The call sheet read as follows: 4,000 crowd to include: 50 mounted police, plus horses; 200 soldiers; 50 army officers; 50 foot police; 60 sailors; 60 nurses; 300 working-class women; 100 upper-class women; 51 *descamisados*; 20 naval officers; 12 naval police; 300 working-class men; 15 palace guards; 8 pallbearers; 60 navy cadets; 60 army cadets; 300 middle-class women; 300 middle-class men; 100 Aristo men; 100 boys; 100 girls; 200 male background; 200 female background; 1,400 miscellaneous background; gun carriage; coffin; 4 army motorcycles; 2 police motorcycles; 6 Bren carriers; 2 half-track military vehicles; 2 fox tanks; 4 army trucks; CGT float, etc. etc. Miraculously, this giant procession was lined up in the street, ready to film by 10:30 in the morning. We shot for two days and the results are on film to see.

As we rolled onwards through Budapest, the crew continued to complain about everything from the food to the rashes they were getting from the chemicals that the hotel used to clean the sheets, to the rashes they were getting in unmentionable areas due to the toilet paper (usually experienced with newsprint on it), to working a seven-day week because of the schedule changes created by promised locations suddenly becoming unavailable. In Hungary, like so many countries that have survived under the communist boot, telling the truth, like democracy, has to be learned all over again. We had hoped to film in Budapest's Catholic basilica, but suddenly were refused to shoot inside, even though they had already allowed us to film the exterior some nights before. It seemed that they had survived the years of Nazi occupation, the '56 uprising, and 45 years of communist, atheist oppression, but couldn't risk our film crew going in there for a couple of hours. Maybe one of the bishops had got his hands on a copy of Madonna's book, *Sex*. We will never know. At least our substantial location fee could have been used to help stop the cathedral from decaying after a century of neglect, crumbling—like most of Budapest—into the street below. Unlike the rest of the buildings in Budapest, its salvation can't be a transformation into a McDonald's.

The Hungarian press didn't help matters either. Too stupid and unworldly to be called capricious, they had shot themselves in the foot with a "supposed" interview with Madonna. Desperate for a homegrown story that was remotely interesting to the rest of the world, they filed their story in "Hunglish" on the wire. Garry Trudeau wickedly "reported" it in *Time* magazine (excerpt):

Blikk magazine: There is so much interest in you from this geographic region, so I must ask this final questions: How many men have you dated in bed? Are they No. 1? How are they comparing to Argentine men who are famous for being on tops as well?

Madonna: Well, to avoid aggravating global terrorism, I would say it's a tie (laughs). No, no I am serious now. See here, I have been working like a canine all the way around the clock. I have been too busy to try the goulash that makes your country one for the record books.

Blikk magazine: Thank you for your candid chit chat.

Madonna: No problem friend, who is a girl.

After five weeks of shooting, we left Hungary. As is apparent from the above, it wasn't a moment too soon for any of us.

Back in London, in the comfort of Shepperton Studios, with most of the crew sleeping in their own beds (and without getting a rash), things were suddenly very civilized. We were in a cozy, controllable environment of English studio sound stages, where the greatest problem, apart from adjusting the schedule for Madonna's pregnancy (and Antonio's wedding), was getting the crew away from the Guinness in the studio bar and back to an afternoon's work.

And so we finished filming at 2 AM on the morning of May 30. For those interested in the nuts and bolts of film making, I would like to give a few statistics on the shooting of *Evita*.

We had filmed for 84 days, shooting in 3 different countries, involving over 600 film crew. We had done 299 scenes and 3,000 slated shots on 320,000 feet of film with 2 cameras. There is no digital multiplication of crowd scenes in the film. Everything was created and shot in camera. Penny Rose's costume department, with a staff of 72 in three different countries, had fitted 40,000 extras in period dress. Over 5,500 costumes were used from 20 different costume houses in London, Rome, Paris, New York, Los Angeles, San Francisco, Buenos Aires and Budapest, including over 1,000 military uniforms. Madonna's wardrobe alone consisted of 85 changes, 39 hats, 45 pairs of shoes and 56 pairs of earrings. Almost all of these were handmade in London. Martin Samuel, our chief hairstylist, created 42 different hair designs for Madonna. Brian Morris' art department created 320 different sets involving 24,000 different items of props. And I could go on. I quote these statistics not only to point out the enormity of the task of making a film of this nature, but to speak up for the scale and effort of the crew involved and to point out that there is still a film industry that doesn't squander money on stupidity, indecision, excess, hubris and Cuban cigars. All this—plus the wonderful work fueled by the imagination, professionalism and passion of film technicians who don't even blink at a 100-hour work week far from home—adds up to the movie we have made.

The many photographs in this book, thanks to our unit photographer David Appleby, I believe accurately represent that movie. I hope you enjoy them.
                                                              —*A l a n   P a r k e r*

LEFT: *Pallbearers carry the coffin up the steps*
of the congress building, where Eva's body will lay in state.

ABOVE: *Narrator Ché (Antonio Banderas)*
sits alone in a Buenos Aires bar commenting on what he sees
as the hysterical reaction to Eva's death.

ABOVE: *The tango singer Agustín Magaldi (Jimmy Nail),
playing in a small cantina in the provincial town of Junín, catches the eye
of young Eva Duarte (Madonna).*

RIGHT: *Eva convinces a reluctant
Magaldi to take her with him to Buenos Aires.*

26

PREVIOUS PAGES: *Eva leaves her hometown of Junín.*

ABOVE: *Eva has her first glimpse of Buenos Aires*
as she arrives at Retiro Railway Station.

RIGHT: *In seedy bars, Eva tastes the reality of life in Buenos Aires*
as she dances with the men of the barrio.

LEFT AND ABOVE: *Eva, penniless and abandoned,*
walks the cobbled streets of La Boca, a working-class area of Buenos Aires.

SINTONIA   EVA DUARTE   FOTO HUEVO

LEFT: *Eva, now an aspiring model and would-be actress, eagerly searches for her photograph in* Sintonía *magazine.*

ABOVE: *Eva's "picture" in* Sintonía—*with cardboard smile and padded bra. (One day the photographer will sell these pictures for a lot of money.)*

ABOVE: *Eva, on the arm of her latest beau,*
Lieutenant Colonel Aníbal Imbert, enjoys the "Hee Leefee"— the
Buenos Aires nightlife.

RIGHT: *Ché, our ever-present narrator,*
continues his realistic and somewhat cynical observations as Eva bounces
up the social ladder with the help of her escorts.

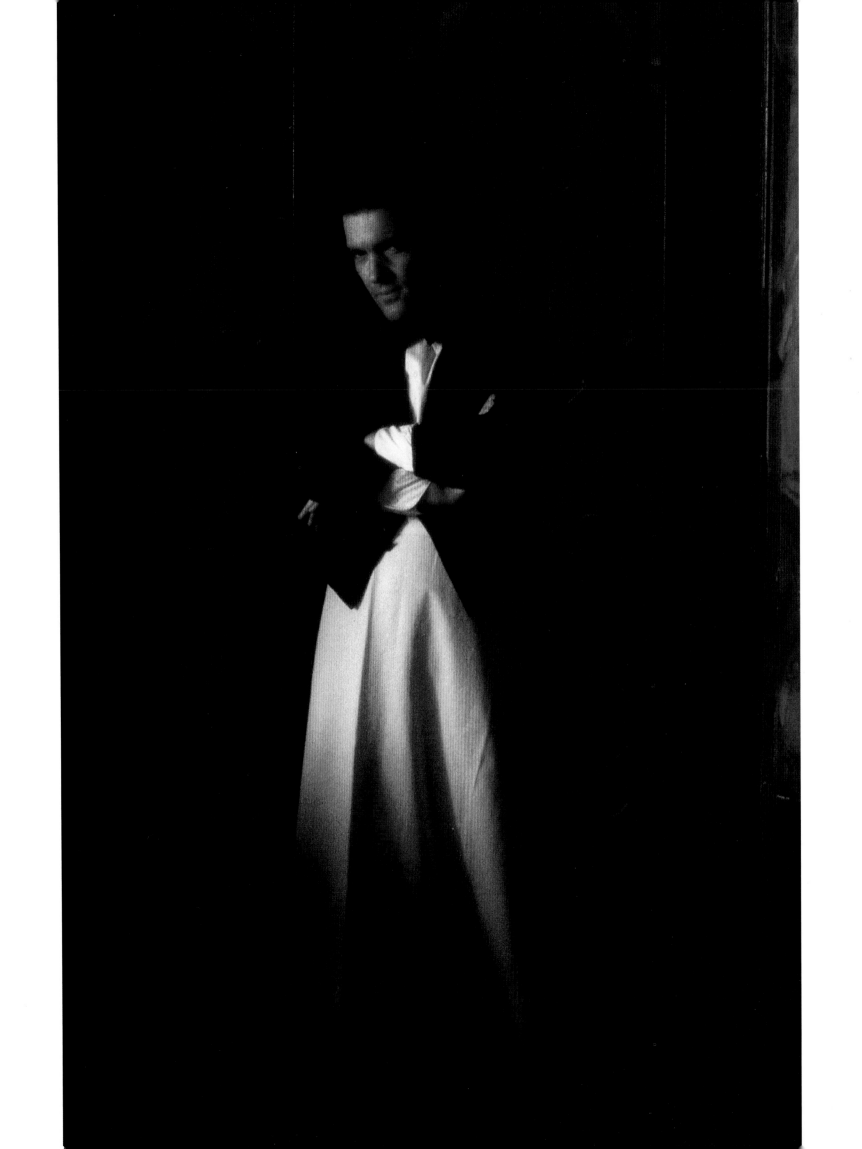

J U A N D O M I N G O P E R O N

On June 4, 1943, a military coup ousted the civilian government of President Ramón Castillo. General Arturo Rawson declared himself President (which, as it turned out, was rather presumptuous, as he only lasted one day, being promptly removed at gunpoint by General Pedro Ramírez).

The political musical chairs was masterminded by a secret military lodge called the GOU, a prominent member of which was a young army colonel, Juan Domingo Perón.

Born in 1895 at Lobos, a province of Buenos Aires, and of Italian descent (Peroni), Perón entered military school at age fifteen. In 1929, now promoted to Captain, he married his first wife, Aurelia Tizón. She died of cancer in 1938. As a Lieutenant Colonel he was sent to Italy in 1939 to observe the Italian army and watched Mussolini speak from the Palazzo Venezia balcony (not the only idea he borrowed from "Il Duce").

Returning from Italy, he took command of the Argentine mountain troops in Mendoza, where he met his young teenage mistress. Just how young she was, and indeed her actual name, is a mystery, it seems, to most historians. Perón paraded her as *mi hija* ("my daughter").

In the military government under General Ramírez, Perón was appointed Under Secretary for War, but also assumed the portfolio of Secretariat of Labor, where he cleverly wooed and embraced the trades unions. Charismatic and handsome, his easy, ingratiating, backslapping style and ready smile inspired the nickname "Colonel Toothpaste." He was equally comfortable drinking with the workers in grimy barrio bars as he was when hobnobbing amongst the braid and gilt of official government functions. Usurping the traditional power base of the socialist left gave him the political springboard from which he would eventually launch his future presidential ambitions.

His political philosophies were a peculiarly Argentinean stew of ideas, embracing socialism, populism and nationalism, borrowing freely (and seemingly randomly) from the British Labour Party, Mussolini and, paradoxically, from the two Joes: Stalin and McCarthy. He eventually coined a new "ism" word for this ideological balancing act—*Justicialismo*, which is apparently (if rather conveniently) untranslatable into English. He believed in the redistribution of wealth away from the rich (particularly away from rich foreigners), government control of the economy, a central bank and distribution of production. All with an unquestioned demagogue, a South American-style *caudillo* (boss) at the helm . . . preferably himself.

LEFT AND ABOVE:

*In January 1944, an earthquake
struck the town of San Juan, 500 miles west
of Buenos Aires.
Many thousands were killed.
Forever the pragmatist,
Perón was not slow to make his presence
felt, nor to miss a photo opportunity,
and turn his publicly aired compassion into
personal political gain.*

ABOVE: *Perón basks in his growing popularity.*

RIGHT: *Meanwhile, Ché has other thoughts as he reflects
on Perón's self-serving political posturing, as the Colonel slides from right
to left and back again.*

LEFT AND ABOVE: *January 22, 1944:*
at a charity concert organized for victims of the San Juan earthquake,
Perón and Eva meet for the first time. She was 24, he 48.

ABOVE AND RIGHT: *Perón's teenage mistress (Andrea Corr) is abruptly shown the door by Eva.*

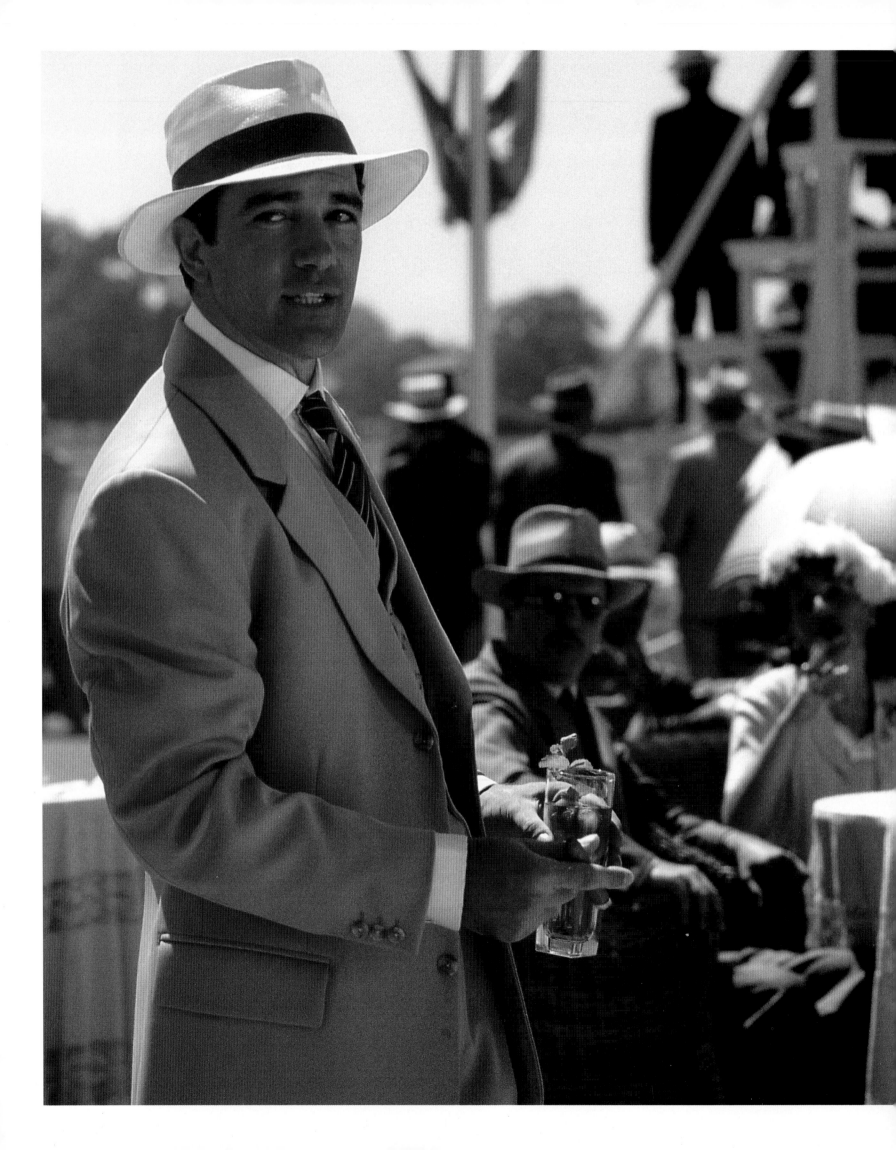

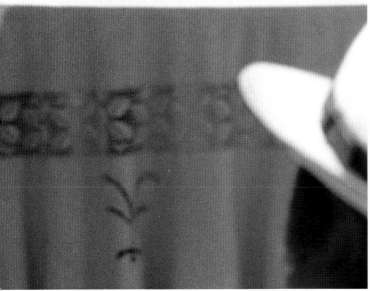

LEFT AND ABOVE: *At the polo fields,
Ché reflects on the less-than-enthusiastic reception by
Buenos Aires society of Perón's actress mistress.*

FOLLOWING PAGES: *In the showers of
the Campo de Mayo garrison, the military echoes its
disapproval of Eva Duarte.*

General Edelmiro Farrell had succeeded Ramírez to the presidency in the bloodless coup of 1944, and named Perón as his vice-president. In March 1945, Farrell handily declared war on Germany and Japan as the Second World War drew to a close. (Argentina was anxious to be on the side of the winners, and so held back any notions of partiality until the victor was certain.) By September of 1945 there was widespread civil unrest in Argentina, and the Campo de Mayo garrison—the seat of military power—put pressure on Farrell to get rid of the uppity, labor-leaning Perón. On October 13, Perón was arrested and incarcerated in the island prison of Martín García. What followed is part Argentine history and part popular Peronist myth. On October 17, Cipriano Reyes, the prominent labor leader, organized a massive, popular uprising that stormed Buenos Aires and culminated in Perón's release. Eva's part in this insurrection was mythologized by Perón and by Eva herself in her book, *The Reason For My Life* (compulsory reading in Argentine schools until the fall of Perón). There is no doubt that prior to these events, Eva, in her privileged position as a popular radio star with thinly-veiled Peronist propaganda programs like "Towards A Better Future," had been a valid and effective political voice. Just how much it can be believed that she was actively involved in the insurrection of October 17 depends, as does so much of Argentinean history, on which side of the Peronist fence people sit and which history book they read.

ABOVE: Eva visits Perón in prison and gives him the strength
to continue fighting for his career.
If he was getting cold feet, she certainly wasn't.

RIGHT: Perón and Eva are reunited after his release from prison.
Not for the last time, Perón yanked off his coat to prove that he was one of the
people: a descamisado.

*Eva and Juan Perón
are married.*

The ceremony probably took place in the small La Plata church of St. Francis in November 1945. The marriage appeared in the register of Eva's hometown of Junín, and there had also been an earlier civil ceremony. The register in Junín had been altered much later as had been the one in her birthplace, Los Toldos, so no historians agree exactly. In the same register, Eva had the surname on her birth certificate altered to show "Duarte," the name she had been using for some time, not the illegitimate "Ibarguren." She also took the opportunity of lopping three years off of her age by changing her birth date to 1922 instead of 1919.

Perón and Eva always said that until then, they had been too busy to get married. What was more accurate was they knew that no Argentinean could run for president while living with a mistress and not a wife.

ABOVE AND RIGHT: *Perón stomps the hinterland in the first democratic elections for sixteen years. Eva accompanied him everywhere— the first time a wife had ever gone with an Argentine politician on the campaign trail. Joining with the trade unions, Perón fought the elections under the "Partido Laborista" banner.*

LEFT: *Ché rescues a small child as violence breaks out at a rally for the Unión Democrática (Perón's opposition).*

Although the elections were independently deemed to be fair, they were not without incident or violence, as both sides did their best to disturb the rallies of the other. Over 100 people were killed as Argentina grappled with democracy. As one observer put it, "the whole of downtown was crying from tear gas." Perón's election train, the *Descamisado*, was derailed after the opposition sawed through an axle. Dr. Tamborini, Perón's opponent, got off lightly—his train was merely stoned and set on fire by Peronist thugs.

ABOVE AND RIGHT: *Argentinean men cast their ballots*
in the elections of February 1946.
(Women did not get the vote in Argentina until 1947.)

71

LEFT AND FOLLOWING PAGES: *Peronist supporters hail Perón's election victory beneath the balcony of the Casa Rosada.*

Perón and the Partido Laborista won the election with 56 percent of the popular vote. They also won the governorship of all 15 provinces and all 30 seats in the Senate. In case anyone got the wrong idea about whose victory it actually was, he soon after renamed the party the "Partido Peronista."

LEFT: *Ché, standing among the crowd in the Plaza de Mayo,*
observes with detached cynicism the massive, theatrical, political spectacle.

ABOVE AND FOLLOWING PAGES: *The crowd's chants for "Perón"*
are gradually drowned out by the growing call for "Evita."
Perón, bemused by this, beckons a reticent Eva to the balcony and the microphones.
A short walk to center stage, where she would remain until her death. And after.

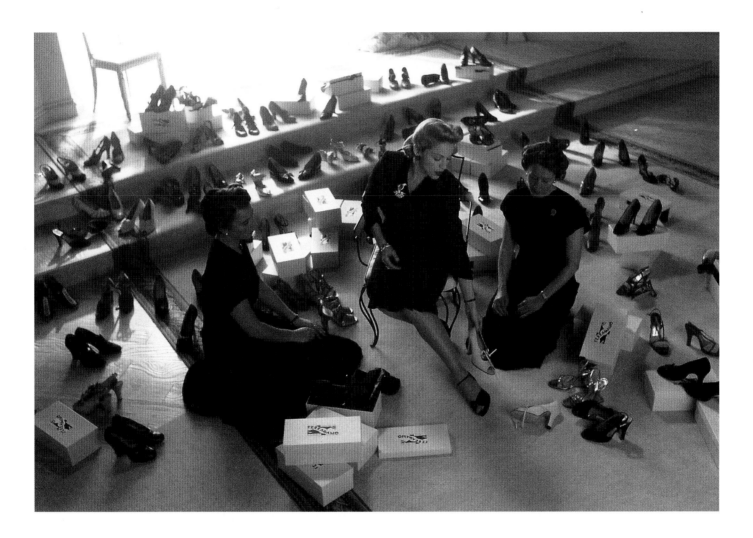

LEFT: *Director Alan Parker and Madonna.*

ABOVE: *Eva throws herself into life as Argentina's first lady
with a media blitz common now but unheard of then.*

PICTURE
POST

HULTON'S
NATIONAL
WEEKLY

THE RAINBOW TOUR
EVA PERON IN EUROPE

JULY 10, 1947

4ᴰ

Vol. 35 No. 11

LEFT AND ABOVE: *In June of 1947,*

Eva embarked on her "Rainbow Tour" of Europe, making headlines in Spain, Italy and France.

In Spain, she was greeted by enormous crowds and a grateful (and until then, internationally friendless)

General Franco, who awarded her with the Grand Cross of Isabel the Catholic.

In Rome, her reception was somewhat cooler as the crowds, with recent memories of Mussolini,

reacted negatively to such demagoguery. However, she still was granted an audience with

Pope Pius XII, who presented her with the perfunctory gift of a rosary.

Eva had expected something more substantial.

LEFT AND ABOVE: *Perón, like millions of his fellow Argentines, was hungry for news of Eva's "Rainbow Tour." Well, the good news at least.*

LEFT AND ABOVE: *Returning from Europe and*
discarding her frivolous image forever,
Eva throws herself into the work of her charitable organization,
"La Fundación Ayuda Social María Eva Duarte de Perón."

PREVIOUS PAGES AND ABOVE: *In July of 1949, Eva formed the "Peronist Women's Party," mobilizing the female vote after suffrage was granted in 1947. Eva campaigned vigorously and soon the Women's Party had 500,000 members and 3,600 branches across the country. Their votes were later a major factor in Perón's re-election victory in November of 1951.*

LEFT: *Parker and Madonna discuss a last-minute script adjustment for Eva's speech to the Peronista women.*

PREVIOUS PAGES, LEFT AND ABOVE: *As the public face of Peronism still was reflected in the media with toothpaste smiles and euphoric, adoring crowds, the economic and social realities were quite different.*

Argentina's once-considerable gold reserves had dwindled during Perón's tenure, and were now at an all-time low. Nationalizing the formerly British-owned railways had been an economic disaster, resulting in widespread strikes of railway workers. Even beef, Argentina's largest export, had to be rationed domestically. Inflation ran rife. (If the Peróns wanted money, they just printed it.) Supreme Court judges and university rectors and teachers unsympathetic to the Peronist cause were replaced by partisans. *La Prensa*, a venerable, conservative and independent newspaper, felt the bite of Perón's growing authoritarianism and was crippled by the government and then forced to close.

ABOVE: *Eva collapses while receiving communion.*

Seemingly oblivious to the violence in the streets, Eva's public deification continued. But in January 1950, the public first became aware of her growing ill health when she collapsed at a meeting of the taxi drivers' union. Her doctor, Oscar Ivanissevich, performed tests and diagnosed uterine cancer.

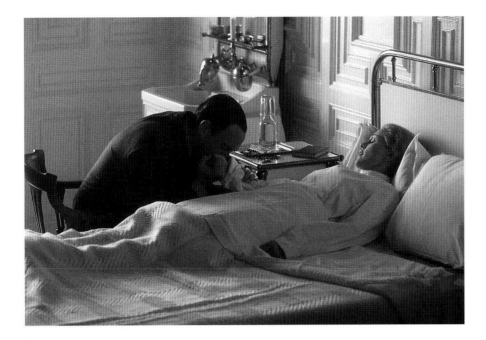

Eva and her tormentor, Ché, unite in their delirium.

ABOVE: *Perón tells Eva that she is dying.*

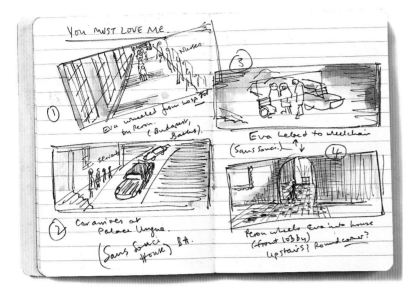
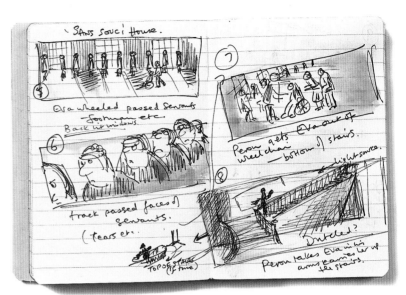
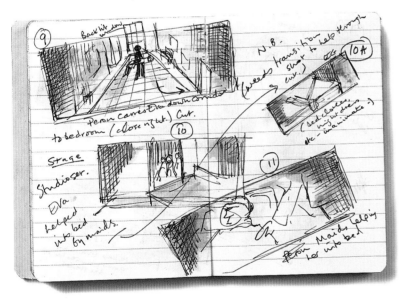

LEFT: *Pages from Alan Parkers's notebooks.*

ABOVE AND FOLLOWING PAGES:

*Perón brings Eva home from the Policlinico to the Palacio Unzué and faces the
personal and political realities of life without her.*

LEFT AND ABOVE: *Despite an overwhelmingly popular, emotional outpouring of support for her candidacy, Eva suddenly, and dramatically, renounces all claims to the vice-presidency and any other political ambitions.*

PREVIOUS PAGES:

Women hold vigil for Eva.

RIGHT: *Ché, at the gates of the Palacio Unzué,*
awaits the news of Eva's death.

ABOVE AND FOLLOWING PAGES:
Ordinary people dance milonga—*a slow, anguished*
but beautiful tango. Collective grief is felt in every
movement of this national dance.

112

As Eva's body lays in state, Perón and Ché bid their last farewells.

ABOVE: *Cinematographer Darius Khondji*
with director Alan Parker.

ACKNOWLEDGMENTS

This book and all the images from the film of *Evita* could not have been possible but for many people. To that end, I would like to thank: Ted Adcock, Luis Alday, Armando Amador-Diaz, David Appleby, Cate Arbeid, Marcelo Auchelli, Simon Baker, Tardy Balazs, David Balfour, Teapot Balseiro, Antonio Banderas, Ignacio Barbe, Clive Barrett, Scott Bates, Tony Bell, Adam Black, Kim Blank, Luis Boccia, Rosa Bologa, Peter Bloor, Sam Bloor, Michele Bock, Pablo Bossi, Judy Bouley, Gary Brooker, Rudi Buckle, John Buckley, Jane Bulmer, Justine Burns, Alan Butler, David Caddick, Kate Carin, Orla Carroll, Jack Carter, Lidia Catalano, Carolyne Chauncey, James Cheek, Peter Childs, Nigel Clay, Colin Codner, Bill Coe, Adam Cooper, Andrea Corr, Christian Cottet, Kenny Crouch, Francesca Crowder, Bob Crowdey, David Cullen, Emma Cullen, Deborah Dalton, Diane Dancklefsen, Richard Daniel, Dennis Davidson, Jake Davies, Yves De Bono, Freddy DeMann, Marc Denize, Yessenia Disla, Florencia Dominguez, Simon Downes, Marcelo Dujovne, Anikó Dunaveczky, Carole Dunne, Joe Dunton, Trevor Dyer, Richard Earl, Emilio Estefan, Rocky Evans, Buzz Feitshans, Erick Feitshans, David Feldman, Lucinda Ferrer, Howard Feuer, Richard Formby, John Gallagher, Julieta Garcia Lenzi, Frank Gardiner, Miranda Garrison, Susie Forte Gilman, Ronald Godard, Pablo Gomez Pereyra, Karen Gonzalez, John Gorham, John Gower, Nickolas Grace, Mark Graham, Rickay Graysmark, Mark Griffin, Alan Grosch, Arthur Guinness, Zsuzsa Gurbán, Annie Hadley, Peter Hall, Gerry Hambling, Ken Hansen, Mike Harris, Nina Hartstone, Sarah Hauldren, John Hay, John Hedges, Paul Hedges, David Henry, Nick Hippisley Coxe, Nick Holder, Mark Holmes, Amy Hubbard, Daniel Hubbard, John Hubbard, Ros Hubbard, Jean-Michel Hugon, Bob Izzard, Sally Jones, Eddy Joseph, Ana Justo, Jacques Kazandjian, Bill Kaye, Darius Khondji, Paddy Kiely, László Kiss, Bob Kocourek, Dr. Alberto Kohan, Kerry Kohler, Gabriel Kraisman, George Kuntner, Greg Kyle, Joan Lader, Wayne Leech, Ailbhe Lemass, Sergio Lerer, Diego Lerner, Ian Lewis, Jane Lewis, Dick Lewzey, Denis Lill, George Little, Julian Littman, Andrew Lloyd Webber, Fernando Lopez, Maria Lujan Hidalgo, Madonna, Dennis Maguire, Bill Mancini, Colin Manning, Alfredo Martin, Marina Marit, John Mauceri, Daniel McCormack, Lee McCutcheon, Alan McPherson, Ray Meehan, President Carlos Menem, Olga Merediz, Mike Moad, Stewart Monteith, Sarah Monzani, Della Moore, Lisa Moran, Brian Morris, Michael Murray, Simon Murray, Barbara Muschietti, Rita Nagy, Jimmy Nail, Andy Nelson, Gordon Neville, Maurice Newsome, Chris Nightingale, Alejandro Nigri, Fernando Nigri, Michelle Noguera, Ashley Nolan, Caresse Norman, John Norster, Norman North, Maria Nunez, Dr. Pacho O'Donnell, Moire O'Sullivan, Laura Pallas, Rosa Maria Parisi, Vincent Paterson, Ricky Pattendon, Randy Paul, Ron Pearce, Pablo Perez Jimenez, Astrid Lund Petersen, Ron Phillips, Thomas Pick, Horacio Pigozzi, Gábor Piroch, Peter Polycarpou, Lisa Anne Porter, Shirley Proctor, Jonathan Pryce, Darren Quinn, Neil Ravan, David Reddaway, Claudio Reiter, Dave Reitzas, Tim Rice, Dave Ridout, Alex Ritchie, Mike Roberts, József Romvári, Penny Rose, Liz Rosenberg, Mark Ryan, Martin Samuel, Mel Sansom, Danny Schwartz, Robin Sellars, Jamie Sewell, Matthew Sharp, J.J. Shea, Libby Shearon, Sandra Shepherd, Zsuzsa Simonyi, Martin Sosa, Szabolcs Stella, Spike Stent, Robert Stigwood, Ian Stone, Victoria Sus, Graham Sutton, Paul Swann, Piroska Szabady, Károly Szekeres, Clarisa Szuszan, Rocky Taylor, Peter Titterell, Gerry Toomey, John Trafford, Philippe Turlure, Joyce Turner, Mária Ungor, Marina Valentini, Andy Vajna, Vando Villamil, Keith Vowles, Derek Wallace, Frederick Warder, David Warren, John Wells, Alan Wertheimer, Ken Weston, Trevor Williams, Roger Willis, Andrew Wilson, David Wimbury, Michael Wimer, Lars Winther, Marcos Woinski, Julia Worsley, Nigel Wright, Ricardo Wullicher, Gabriella Zahorán. — *Alan Parker*

EVA DUARTE DE PERON

1919 — 1952